Gold for Jesus

Gold for Jesus

Phyllis A. Bowen

VANTAGE PRESS
New York

Scriptural notations are from the King James version of the Bible

FIRST EDITION

Published by Vantage Press, Inc.
516 West 34th Street, New York, New York 10001

Manufactured in the United States of America
ISBN: 0-533-11024-6

Library of Congress Catalog Card No.: 94-90008

0 9 8 7 6 5 4 3 2 1

In memory of my pastor, Dr. Charles Haddon Spurgeon Sadaphal, Sr., who acquired much gold for Jesus before he went home to Jesus, **and to His teachings**. The Holy Spirit used Pastor Sadaphal to pray me through many a trial and to teach me the Word of God, always encouraging me with godly counselling to rejoice always, for this is the will of God in Christ Jesus concerning me and that I should give God thanks in all things, always reminding me to keep my eyes upon the Lord and that all things shall work together for my good.

Also to my mother and sisters and brothers and all my family (spiritual and in the flesh), who have encouraged me in the Lord in my times of testings. I thank my Heavenly Father and, most of all, I dedicate this work to my Lord and Saviour Jesus Christ, who has never forsaken me and who fights for me through His Holy Spirit.

I counsel thee to buy of me gold tried in the fire, that thou mayest be rich; and white raiment, that thou mayest be clothed, and that the shame of thy nakedness do not appear, and anoint thine eyes with eyesalve, that thou mayest see.

—Revelation 3:18

Weep thee not
For in the morning cometh rejoicing
For I will lift the darkness
of the night
And cause my glory to
shine before thee
Know that I have never left thee
Nor would I ever forsake thee
For I have loved thee
with an everlasting love
SAITH GOD
(*Prophecy of the Holy Spirit given at Deeper Life Christian Fellowship*)

Contents

Gold for Jesus

Introduction

One evening as I sat writing, my mind was completely focused on my "concerns," and suddenly I became aware of a pencil on my table that had the words written on it, **"Go for the Gold."** I didn't know where the pencil came from. As a matter of fact, I don't remember having seen it before, and as I looked at it, I could not take my eyes off the inscription, **"Go for the Gold."** I knew beyond the shadow of a doubt that the Holy Spirit was speaking directly to me. I began to laugh within myself at God's humor and became so excited over it, so exuberant was I that the Lord Himself was saying to me, "Stop worrying and do what you find so difficult to do. Stop fearing. Press on. Stay in the race. Take authority over the circumstances and **Go for the Gold.**" With profundity and yet with humor He spoke to me, and in the rapture of it all, I remembered the Scripture, *". . . buy of me gold tried in the fire"* (Rev. 3:18), and the Scripture from Ecclesiastes, *"The race is not to the swift but to him who endures."* I was encouraged to continue in the race, endeavoring anew to become as gold for Jesus' sake.

In the following pages are written some thoughts on suffering and on why God allows Christians to suffer. I believe through it all God wants us to endure to the end. He wants to make us a people He can pour His spirit into, a people He can use, a people who will wear the golden crowns of His glory, a people He can hold up to Satan's scrutiny and say, "Consider My servant."

My prayer is that we will be such a people, a people who will **Go for the Gold for Jesus**.

GOD SO LOVED

Picture by
Curtis

God's Plan to Send His Son for Redemption of Mankind to Erase the Curse of Sin

This earth is a place of testing, where we spend a very short time to prepare us for the place where our souls will spend eternity. Almighty Jehovah God put man here to be in fellowship with Him, but man disobeyed God and sinned, thereby receiving the curse of God. God still wanted fellowship with man because of His great love for His creation, whom He created in His own image, but although He allowed man to continue to live upon this earth, after Adam sinned, man could no longer live in the abundance of blessings that God had planned.

However, God had another plan—a great plan to send His only begotten Son to earth so that whosoever desired it could become like His Son and live forever in the blessings of God (Gen. 12:3 and John 3:16).

When Adam sinned and man fell from grace, God's plan to send His Son to redeem the earth began to unfold. There are numerous scriptures throughout the Old and the New Testaments prophesying and portraying this plan of God to send His Son. In the fifth chapter of Romans, the Holy Spirit clearly shows this plan:

Wherefore, as by one man sin entered into the world, and death by sin . . . For if by one man's offence death reigned by one; much more they which receive abundance of grace and of the gift of righteousness shall reign in life by one, Jesus Christ. Therefore as by the offence of one judgment came upon all men to condemnation; even

3

so by the righteousness of one the free gift came upon all men unto justification of life. For as by one man's disobedience many were made sinners, so by the obedience of one shall many be made righteous.

In the age after the fall of Adam, mankind became very wicked, and in bringing about the beginning of God's great plan to send His son, the earth had to be purged by a great flood, whereby everything was destroyed with the exception of one righteous man and his family because he believed and obeyed God. In Gen. 6:5–8 we see the unfolding of this:

And God saw that the wickedness of man was great in the earth, and that every imagination of the thoughts of his heart was only evil continually. And it repented the Lord that he had made man on the earth, and it grieved him at his heart. And the Lord said, I will destroy man whom I have created man, and beast, and the creeping thing, and the fowls of the air; for it repenteth me that I have made them. But Noah found grace in the eyes of the Lord.

From Noah's family the whole earth was again populated, and God chose a man called Abraham to whom he gave the promise in Gen. 12:2–3: *"And I will make of thee a great nation . . . and in them shall all the families of the earth be blessed,"* and covenanted in Gen. 17:19: *"And God said, Sarah thy wife shall bear thee a son indeed; and thou shalt call his name Isaac; and I will establish my covenant with him for an everlasting covenant, and with his seed after him."*

From Abraham, his son Isaac and Isaac's son Jacob came the race of people God chose to hear His laws and to be an example of how man should walk with God, out of and from whom would come His Son, the promised Messiah. God chose the Israelites, and He chose from among them a man called Moses to lead them. He gave them certain rules and laws to live by, and He told them that if they would live by these rules, they would be His people and He would be their God and they would be blessed and their generations would be blessed. He gave them the Passover and the practice of slaying lambs so that the blood could be used by the high priest to cleanse their sins and so that God could continue to bless them, since He is a holy God and cannot look upon sin and cannot bless sin. He allowed them to go through trials and sufferings in the wilderness to teach them to trust Him and to walk in His ways.

However, in spite of the fact that He took them out of the bondage of slavery in Egypt, opened the Red Sea for them to escape from their enemies, and gave them many miracles as they travelled through the wilderness on the way to the Promised Land, they disobeyed God many times and could not keep His laws perfectly. The sins of mankind became so great that the blood of animals was no longer sufficient to cleanse sins, so Jehovah God brought to pass the fulfillment of His plan to send the promised Messiah, His Son Jesus Christ (John 3:16), to be the ultimate lamb, so that sacred blood could be shed, not only for the Israelites, but for all mankind. *"Without the shedding of blood there is no remission of sin."*

When we ask God's forgiveness of our sins, reminding Him that the blood of His Son has been shed for us, He forgives us our sins. But if we don't, He cannot forgive us. We have to humbly ask forgiveness in the name of His Son Jesus Christ. We have to, above all things, recognize the great sacrifice our heavenly Father, Jehovah God, made for us when He sent His Son, "the Bright and Morning Star," to this earth to suffer and shed His blood for us so that His Holy Spirit can live in us and sin can be erased when we repent and invite His Son into our hearts. *"Verily, verily I say unto thee, Except a man be born again he cannot see the kingdom of God* (John 3:3)."

Only with the Son of God living in our hearts can we overcome sin and the temptations of the serpent who beguiled Eve and brought original sin into the world. Only with the Son of God living in our hearts can we hope to strive to be like golden vessels fit for the master's use. Only with the Son of God living in our hearts can

5

we run the race of life and become more than conquerors. Only with the Son of God living in our hearts can we be strong in the face of suffering, as we run the race to victory and **go for the gold** for Jesus because the Saviour Himself commands us: *"Buy of me gold tried in the fire."*

God Allows Christians to Suffer—Why?

We Have to Be Tested

We often ask, "Why does God allow Christians to suffer?" We will be tried and tested. Even Jesus Christ was tested. It's through testings that we grow strong and become as He wants us to be for He said, *"As my Father has sent me so send I you."* In Ecclesiastes it is written: *"To every thing there is a season, and a time to every purpose under the Heaven: A time to be born, and a time to die; a time to plant and a time to pluck up . . . A time to weep and a time to laugh . . ."* We have to have the rain so that the flowers will grow. Suffering always brings some good. The ultimate good is that we should come nearer to God. If we never had a problem, we would not know that He could solve them.

Someone said, "The trials that we have each day are merely stepping stones and help us to rely on Him and trust in Him alone." Paul said, *"And we know that all things work together for good to those who love the Lord."* All stepping stones are laid together for good to those who love the Lord. Very often, in order for God to take us from one point of our lives to another, we have to go through certain irritating or sorrowful things. But as we go through those things, doing God's will, we become like the pearl (as my pastor reminds us) that is created into the beautiful priceless jewel, as it is rubbed (irritated) over and over again, in an oyster shell that lies in the moving waters on the ocean bed, for a very long period of time.

I heard a minister say that while it only takes six months to grow squash, an oak tree takes many, many years to grow tall and

7

strong (one hundred years). God wants us to be like the oak, not like the squash. And out of every irritating and obnoxious situation that enters our lives and that seems to go on for long periods of time, the Lord wants to bring something beautiful, of a sweet-smelling savor, something strong and wonderful that He can point to as His trophies, as His priceless jewels. In the Book of Revelation, the Lord Jesus Christ tells the church to buy gold tried in the fire, and in Job it is written: *"When he has tried me I shall come forth as gold"* (Job 23:10). God wants us to be His spiritual gold.

Buy Gold in the Wilderness

Every child of God has his or her wilderness experience from time to time. It seems that to attain some cherished goal one always has to fight the Canaanites and take the land by force in order to reach that goal. It seems that we travel the route of the Israelites, spiritually speaking, from the moment we're born again. However, it's in the wilderness situations that the gold of the spirit is acquired.

Every Christian must leave Egypt, and there is always the crossing of the Red Sea. It's interesting to remember that the Red Sea will not open until your back is against the wall. When the Israelites were running away from the Egyptians, they came to a place where the only thing facing them was the Red Sea. They had to accept Moses' faith that God would part the Red Sea for them to go over to the other side.

Sometimes when we're facing adverse circumstances and people are telling us things like, "It's always darkest before the dawn," "Joy comes in the morning," "There is a silver lining behind every cloud," etc., we tend to think, "Oh, really! Well, show me, where is the sunshine, where is the silver lining!" and "How long must I go through this," and "My back is up against the wall!"

However, when we show faith and trust in God, it's exactly at this time when God often comes through, opens a door, and makes a way. When our backs are against the wall, He causes the Red Sea to part so that we can receive deliverance and cross over to the side of sunshine. And later, looking back on that difficult situation, you may realize that you now have the **gold of strength** in your spirit.

A minister at my church pointed out that we don't have to suffer in the wilderness for forty years as the Israelites did. The Israelites took forty years because of lack of faith that they could take the land when God first brought them near to Canaan. If we trust God, our stay in the wilderness may be shortened considerably. But spiritually speaking, we often go through the wilderness with all its experiences, its disappointments, and its sufferings, and it really does seem that you cannot enjoy and appreciate your promised land until you've gone through the fires of life and have been tested in the wilderness. Paul reminds us in 1 Cor. 3:13: *"Every man's work shall be made manifest for the day shall declare it, because it shall be revealed by fire and the fire shall try every man's work of what sort it is."*

As we go through life, with changing of goals, we go through toward one promised land and then another. Our ultimate promised land is Heaven, the glorious New Jerusalem; and all our sufferings upon this earth, as we go through various fires and trials, can be said to be our travels through the wilderness, on our way to that glorious place. God says:

> I counsel thee to buy of me gold tried in the fire, that thou mayest be rich; and white raiment, that thou mayest be clothed, and that the shame of thy nakedness do not appear, and anoint thine eyes with eyesalve, that thou mayest see (Rev. 3:18).

It is in the wilderness experiences which suffering brings, that we learn to become spiritual athletes. It is then that we learn to keep our eyes always on the Lord as we press forward and run for the gold. With the increasing evils of the world, as last-day children of God, we have to be prepared to sometimes overcome seemingly insurmountable obstacles as we jump through the hoops and over the traps that the devil sets for us in each trial of our wilderness experiences. Yes, it is in this wilderness experience that we may acquire the gold that has been tried in the fires of life and bring and present this gold of the spirit to Jesus.

Thank God for Pressure

I read the following paragraph in a *Daily Word* book:

A young boy was fascinated to see the stirrings of life in a cocoon. The moth inside was struggling to free itself, but the process was slow and tedious. Thinking he would help the moth, he slit the cocoon with his pocketknife, and the insect emerged freely. But it had none of the expected color, it couldn't fly, and it soon died. The boy later learned that a moth's struggle to free itself is a necessary part of its development, and that the process stimulates body fluids that give luster to its wings.

The pressure to help our loved ones when we see them struggling can be agonizing sometimes. But like the young boy who helped free the moth from the cocoon and instead inadvertently brought death to the moth, so we, if we do not let go of our loved ones, allowing them to learn to fly, allowing them to go through the pressure situations themselves, will cause harm to come to them instead of help.

The Lord has shown me this many times concerning my children, how I must let go and let them develop character, how I must let go and let God. And I've seen in the times when I have obeyed God, how things worked out better for them than if I had persisted in helping them. Tough love is a difficult thing to practice, but when we consider that it's better to obey God than to have our children's lives go all wrong, we see we have no choice. So praise God for the pressure that suffering in growth brings.

Thank God for Pain!

After I read a book called *Where Is God When It Hurts?* I realized something very interesting about pain. If we didn't have pain, we wouldn't be warned of impending danger. Pain is actually a gift from God to protect and to warn us of and to preserve us from dangers of all kinds. That's why Hansen's disease, leprosy, is called a "painless hell." Philip Yancey in his book states:

> Hansen's disease (HD) is cruel, but not at all the way other diseases are. It primarily acts as an anesthetic, numbing the pain cells of hands, feet, nose, ears, and eyes. . . . Most diseases are feared because of their pain. . . . Hansen's disease's numbing quality is precisely the reason such fabled destruction and decay of tissue occurs. For thousands of years people thought HD caused the ulcers on hands and feet and face which eventually led to rotting flesh and loss of limbs. Mainly through Dr. Brand's research, it has been established that in 99 percent of the cases, HD only numbs the extremities. The destruction follows solely because the warning system of pain is gone. . . . A person with HD has been known to reach directly into a charcoal fire to retrieve a dropped potato. Nothing in his body told him not to.

The person with HD who put his hand in the fire and could not feel the pain still received the burns on his hands and perhaps suffered the loss of his fingers. This disease causes people to destroy themselves due to the lack of a warning pain to alert them or the muffling of painful sensations. People with this disease can hold a sharp object and not feel the sensation of pressure to the hand, or step on a sharp object and not know they're hurt until they see themselves bleeding.

So we can thank God for the gift of pain that warns us of danger. Pain is a necessary part of our lives on this earth. If we're to know that some part of our bodies needs healing, we're alerted by pain. In the same way, emotional pain warns us that something is wrong in our soul and needs fixing, needs the deliverance power of the Balm of Gilead. When we seek the Balm of Gilead, we come near to God, so we can thank God for pain.

The Pride of Life

God knows what kinds of suffering it takes for each of his children to be humbled and to do what His will is for our lives. But the strongman of pride can stop us from getting God's perfect will in our lives, and through disobedience caused by pride we may go through our entire lives never experiencing the fulfillment of God's perfect will for our lives. We may touch on it but never really fulfill it. So God allows certain situations to come into our lives to kill the pride, so to speak (crucify the flesh), and pride is what God wants to cast out and remove completely from all of us who are His children when He allows various kinds of evil situations to humble our lives. (Prov. 16:18: **"Pride goeth before destruction, and an haughty spirit before a fall."**)

Pride is the strongman of all evil. It's through pride that rebellion exists. When Lucifer lifted himself up against God in Heaven, it was pride that caused him to do so (Isa. 14:12–13). It was pride that caused him to rebel against God. It was pride that caused him to fall from Jehovah's high and holy Heaven. He said he wanted to be like the most high God (Isa. 14:14: **I will ascend above the heights of the clouds, I will be like the most high**). Job was stripped of all pride by the end of his sufferings. (Job 40:4: **Behold, I am vile; what shall I answer thee? I will lay mine hand upon my mouth.**) (Job 42:6: **Wherefore I abhor myself, and repent in dust and ashes.**)

The Lord has to discourage us from holding a proud and haughty spirit by instilling humility into us. God knows what kind of suffering it takes for each one of His children to be cleansed of pride, yielded to Him and walking in humility. So each person's suffering is different. The situation it takes to revile one person may not humble someone else.

Humility does not mean weakness. Humility has great strength. (Phil. 2:6–10: **Who being in the form of God, thought it not robbery to be equal with God: But made himself of no reputation, and took upon him the form of a servant, and was made in the likeness of men: And being found in fashion as a man, he humbled himself, and become obedient unto death, even the death of the cross.**) Jesus Christ walked with complete humility and all who follow Him must do the same. Humble people are gentle people with a touch of greatness. I like what David said in the eighteenth chapter of the Psalms: **"Thy gentleness has made me great!"**

Scripture tells us that the Pride of Life is not of the Father but is of the world (1 John 2:16). He wants us to be without a spot or a wrinkle of pride from the world when He comes for His bride, the Church.

GOD SO LOVED

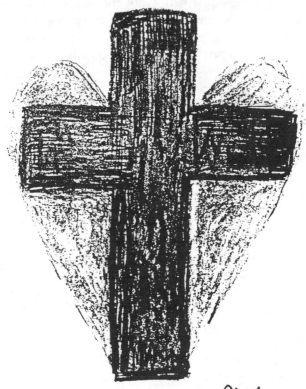

Picture by
Curtis

God Takes Us Through

God Carries us

Someone had a dream of footprints in the sand and of seeing two sets of footprints changing to one set of footprints at certain points in her life. In the dream, God told her that when she saw only one set of footprints, He had not forsaken her, but that He was "carrying her" at her most troubling times in life. Many times we look back and say, "I don't know how I did it" or "I don't know how I got through that," but the truth is that we did not do it. The truth is that God did it. God carried us through in the wilderness experiences of our lives as He carried the Israelites through the wilderness. He said, *"I bore you on eagles' wings and brought you to myself. Now, therefore, if you will indeed obey my voice and keep my covenant, then you shall be a special treasure to me above all people, for all the earth is mine."*

Walking on Water

God yearns for our fellowship and comes running across our deep seas to our rescue when we say, "Father, I have sinned, forgive me. I want Jesus Christ to live in me and show me the way and help me to gain strength and deliverance in these trials." Peter did not sink when he walked on the water—he was only beginning to sink and he cried out to Jesus and Jesus saved him.

So the Lord comes running across our rough waters when we

cry out in our despair and when our boat is seemingly tempest tossed and sinking! He stretches out His hands and says, "Come," and as we walk upon the rough waters of our deep seas toward Him, fixing our eyes upon Jesus, the author and finisher of our faith, He gently looks at us and says, "Take my pillow and rest in me."

Thank God that even while we say, "Lord, I'm sorry, forgive me," He doesn't see the despair and hopelessness that we see, but He sees in our hearts that we desire to become what he desi ɔ us to be. Thank God that He doesn't see us as we see ourselves but that He sees beyond and that He looks not at the surface but at the heart of the person. He sees the yearning, the desire to be His servant, to please Him, the desire to walk continually in His spirit, the desire to walk on the water when He bids us come to Him. We long to run to Jesus, going for the spiritual gold so that he may make us golden vessels fit for His use, vessels that will not leak, but vessels that will hold His spirit.

Going Through

Deliverance is received while we're going through the fire, while we're actually in the fire, when the fire is purifying us, burning out the dross and making us like gold—not after we've gone through and not after the fire but during the fire, and when we learn to become overcomers while we're learning to overcome. That's why we must go through. In Isaiah the prophet writes: *"Go through, go through the gates, prepare ye the way of the people; cast up, cast up the highway; gather out the stones; lift up a standard for the people"* (Isa. 62:10). And the Lord assures His people that *". . . when the enemy shall come in like a flood the spirit of the Lord shall lift up a standard."* He also assures us that *"when thou passeth through the waters, I will be with thee; and through the rivers, they shall not overflow thee; when thou walkest through the fire thou shall not be burned; neither shall the flame kindle upon thee"* (Isa. 43:2). It's always as we're going through some kind of suffering that we receive deliverance. We can't be delivered from our foes if we turn and run. We have to stand, holding up the standard of the sword of the spirit, the Word of God, and go forward—"Onward, Christian Soldiers." Onward!

As Christians, while we're upon this earth, we can expect to go through many storms, tests and trials; and as the time comes nearer for Jesus to come, the roaring devil and his demons become more vicious, but Jesus has said that He is with us always; He will never leave us and we are more than conquerors.

One of God's great pilots, Kathryn Kuhlman, once said, "Great pilots are made in rough waters and deep seas" and another one of God's great pilots upon this earth, my pastor, Rev. Charles Sadaphal, Sr., said, "When you go through the storms of life, like the eagle, go above the storms in praise and thanksgiving." And a sister in the Lord said, "God will take us through; it's how we go through that's important." My pastor tells us that to go through the storms, we should go above the storms. He tells us to do this by looking unto Jesus from whence comes our redemption, keeping our eyes upon Him, rejoicing and singing and praying His name (for at the name of Jesus every knee shall bow, even the knees of the demons who plague our souls), and above all blessing and praising Him.

Pastor reminds us of what the word says concerning reigning—that we should reign in life through Christ Jesus. He also tells us that we should go above the storms by letting the high praises of God be in our mouths and the two-edged sword in our hands—by living the 149th Psalm, by rejoicing and always practicing joy, because a Christian is like a soldier in enemy territory and must always have on the armor of God to withstand satan's tricks, lies, and devices.

The apostle Paul commands us to put on the whole armor of God and arm ourselves like a solider ready for battle, putting on the breastplate of righteousness, the helmet of salvation, having our

17

feet shod with peace, holding the sword of the spirit in our hands, and having on the shield of faith, praying always with all prayer and supplication in the spirit for the saints (Eph. 6:10–13).

If we go through like this, victory is truly assured. (Deliverance may not come right away, because the length of a test is not always short, but victory can be experienced in our spirits if we go through the way God commands us to.) But very often in our human frailties we don't take the advice of God's great pilots and we fall into a lot of trouble while going through tests and trials.

But God is faithful to encourage us in all our trials; and through all the confusing clamor of fear, anger, accusations, misunderstandings, intimidation, condemnation, hurts, bitterness, Jesus whispers to us, "I have not forsaken you," "Trust me," "Higher," "Come closer to me," "Rejoice," "Faith, have faith in me," "Be still and know that I am God," and He assures us "I will fight for you." Sometimes in our dilemma we may cry out, "O God! Why!" and He may tenderly answer to our tortured souls, "You do not realize now what I'm doing, but later you will understand"; and He goes ahead of us and prepares a table for our feast in the presence of our enemies by opening up surprising doors and windows of blessings and miracles in the midst of the trials. He spreads a table in our wilderness experience. Then we get on our knees and ask for mercy for having shown such lack of faith and say, "O Lord, I love you. Thank you for the blessings and even thank you for the trials. Just stay by my side, Jesus, and I'll hold onto your hand and I'll go through anything you want me to, Lord! But help me not to wander away from your sheepfold, Lord." As it is written in Job 13:15: *"Though he slay me, yet will I trust in him: but I will maintain mine own ways before him."*

When the running becomes tiring, and we can't see our way as we go through, and the victory is hidden by the devil's lies and torments, we can take heart in the realization that the real gold medal champion is living right inside of us and we just have to call upon Him and speak His name—"JESUS"—and He will immedi-

18

ately give us added strength and encouragement for the journey. He'll say, "Keep running and go for the gold, for I'm always with you and I will not forsake you."

Christ Redeems Us from the Curse of the Law

One of God's rules has always been that someone has to pay for sin and that the sins of the fathers are sent down to the children and other generations. However, because of the shedding of God's blood, the blood of Jesus Christ is able to break all curses of our past and release us from the sins of our forefathers, provided we believe on Jesus and ask for forgiveness and repent of our own sins. When we come to Jesus, we are born again, and seek His sanctification in our lives, this happens—the sins of our forefathers are washed away from our lives. "Christ redeems us from the curse of the law." But we have to ask for this forgiveness, and God then gives us the greatest gift of all, the gift of salvation.

The nations of this world that have forsaken and neglected Jesus Christ and what Jesus stands for in the way of love and forgiveness, and that refuse to take this gift of salvation through Jesus Christ, are the nations that suffer greatly in this day and age and are always at war, for they reject God's greatest gift of salvation through Jesus Christ. They reject the redemption that the blood of Jesus gives and in doing so, automatically accept the curse of the law.

The Lord Thy God Shall Circumcise Thy Heart

When we come to the Lord, we have to go through a time of circumcision of the heart to come to a place of sanctification. This can only be accomplished through trials and testing, or "suffering" if you will. The Lord saved my soul in 1978 when I became born again, and in 1982 He gave me the following promise: *"And the Lord thy God shall circumcise thy heart and the heart of thy seed to love the Lord thy God with all thy heart and with all thy soul that thou mayest live"* (Deut. 30:6).

I claimed this promise wholeheartedly, especially as it concerned my seed, but I did not fully realize its meaning until, after having gone through many tests and trials, I heard a message at church, on November 1990, concerning circumcision of the heart. Then I realized, "Yes, Lord, that's what you've been doing—circumcising my heart—so that I may live—live the abundant, reigning, victorious life in this life and live with you eternally (especially); and that my children also may live."

Tailor-made Suffering

We sometimes wonder why God gives certain types of sufferings to some and not to others, but as I heard a minister say, "All suffering is tailor-made to suit each believer." One person may look at another person's situation and say, "I could never stand that. I couldn't take it. I don't know how you do it"; while their own situation is just as bad or seemingly worse from the other person's viewpoint. It seems that the stronger a Christian is, the closer one is to God—the harder the devil comes against you. I suppose that, because Satan knows he can't get at God's true servants with small thorns, he deals with them more fiercely. Also, it would seem that the more teachings one has received, the greater the trials may be at the time of testing if the knowledge from those teachings is not used, for it is written, *"To whom much is given much is expected."*

So the Lord knows what each of us can bear in our respective situations and how to suit our respective personalities and lives. Most of all, He knows how to bring to pass what He wants to do in each one of our lives. He gives us grace to accept and endure what we never thought we could, until He brings us through like shining gold. He gives grace, His grace is sufficient. Thank God for His grace. Thank God for Jesus!

Not Necessarily Because of Sin

We often think that we must have committed some great sin or even the unpardonable sin to be in the predicament we're in. We often say, "Lord, what did I do to deserve this?" However, in John 9:3, the Lord said, **"Neither hath this man sinned, nor his parents: but that the works of God should be made manifest in him."** And in John 11:4, the Lord said, **"This sickness is not unto death, but for the glory of God that the Son of God might be glorified thereby."**

We see really good people suffering greatly and one can't help but ask, "Why, Lord?!" I once heard a minister say, "Grace has to have a place within which grace can work and redeeming love has to have an arena wherein which to operate." I thought, "How true." God often allows misfortune, hardships, or illness, so that His great grace and wonderful love can be seen clearly; so that we can see and know that this miracle of deliverance or healing comes about by no means of our own but solely and completely through the power of the Holy Spirit. Sometimes the miracle doesn't come in the form of immediate deliverance but manifests in the way in which we come through a situation, as we learn in the situation and experience the grace of God flowing through our lives to bring us joyfully and victoriously through this time of growth. We learn to wait upon God, so that His grace clearly comes through in such situations.

We see in the miracle of Lazarus being raised from the dead how Jesus, deliberately it seems, waited two days before proceeding on His journey to raise Lazarus from the dead. I guess we can say the Lord made sure Lazarus was "really dead" before bringing about this miracle. In this way there could be no doubt that it was a miracle from God and that God was given all the glory. In Judges, when Gideon amassed an army to fight the Midianites and Amalekites, we see how God told Gideon to reduce his army to only three hundred fighting men **". . . lest Israel vaunt themselves against me, saying, Mine own hand hath saved me."** Here God's love for the Children of Israel could be clearly seen by them when, with only three hundred men, they conquered the thousands of Midianites and Amalekites. They would clearly see that their victory came about not through any power or strength of their own, but because God fought for them. This was God's arena, at this time, wherein His redeeming love could operate.

When we're tempted to say "Why?" we can also reflect on Deuteronomy 29:29: **"The secret things belong unto the Lord our God. . . ."** When we see those who are not healed or not healed in our time, not healed "now," we often say to God, "Do it NOW, Lord," but God has His own timetable. He tells us that His thoughts are not our thoughts and His ways are not our ways. I suppose if we were to know everything that God is going to do at a future time, we would not wait upon Him with such intensity, and more importantly our faith would not be exercised. We do not know everything; the secret things belong unto the Lord. Our sufferings are not always because of sin. Certainly Job's sufferings were not because he had committed sin, in spite of what his friends said to him, but simply because God allowed Satan to test him at that time of his life.

Paul says, "This is the will of God in Christ Jesus concerning you." Sometimes it is God's will that we stay in a certain situation for what may seem to us to be "forever." But God **"will not allow us to be tempted more than we're able and will with the temptation make a way of escape."** He reminds us that **"my grace is sufficient for my strength is made perfect in weakness."** He will not give us more than we can bear. He's constantly watching over us. As we let go of our own strength and rely on God's strength, becoming weak so that God's strength may work, letting go and letting God, we begin to see His power work, and we gain deliverance and victory in the situation. We use each trial as a stepping stone to where God wants to take us. We become the priceless pearl of God. We become priceless through learning to be an overcomer and God's victor in the fires and trials of life. **"The steps of a righteous man are ordered by the Lord."** As we press on to that higher ground in the spirit, we have to be also prepared to run for the spiritual gold—to go for the gold and to get the gold for Jesus' sake.

During the course of a very evil trial that came upon my life, I asked the Lord, "Why?" Because to the outward appearance, it would seem that I must have committed some great sin and when I looked back upon the last ten to twelve years since receiving salvation I remembered the sins of disobedience and rebellion in not carrying out the Holy Spirit's instructions as He had given them to me and I saw how this disobedience was a great sin, for He said to whom much is given much is expected no matter how great the cost, and I had been given much. However, to my question of "why" the Lord replied, **"I am giving you a testimony."** After thinking about it clearly, I rejoiced, because I knew then that the Lord was giving me a chance to become silver and gold in the Kingdom of Heaven and not remain as wood, stubble, and hay. And God promised to give me something!

Overcoming

Silver and gold are only for overcomers, so the Lord is giving me a chance to become an overcomer, for the great promises in Revelation start with "He that overcomes . . ." where the Lord gives us these tremendous and awesome promises:

Rev. 2:7: To him that overcometh will I give to eat of the tree of life, which is in the midst of the paradise of God.

Rev. 2:11: He that overcometh shall not be hurt of the second death.

Rev. 2:17: To him that overcometh will I give to eat of the hidden manna, and will give him a white stone, and in the stone a new name written, which no man knoweth saving he that receiveth it.

Rev. 2:26: And he that overcometh and keepeth my works unto the end, to him will I give power over the nations.

Rev. 3:5: He that overcometh, the same shall be clothed in white raiment; and I will not blot his name out of the book of life, but I will confess his name before my Father and before his angels.

Rev. 3:12: Him that overcometh will I make a pillar in the temple of my God, and he shall go no more out; and I will write upon him the name of my God and the name of the city of my God, which is new Jerusalem, which cometh down out of heaven from my God; and I will write upon him my new name.

Rev. 3:21: To him that overcometh will I grant to sit with me in my throne, even as I also overcame and am sat down with my Father in his throne.

Rev. 21:7: He that overcometh shall inherit all things; and I will be his God, and he shall be my son.

So each trial helps to build up our spiritual bank account in Heaven, for as we overcome, God gives us something. And what a SOMETHING!

When we overcome, we are given to eat of the tree of life; we shall not be hurt of the second death; we will be given to eat of the hidden manna; we will be given a white stone and a new name; we will be given power over the nations; we shall be clothed in white raiment; our names will not be blotted out of the book of life, but Jesus will confess our names before His Father and before His angels; Jesus will make us a pillar in the temple of God, and He will write upon us the name of God; Jesus will grant us to sit with Him on His throne; we shall inherit all things; and most of all Jesus will be our God and we shall be His sons and His daughters.

Indeed, that's a great Something that God will give overcomers! And all these Somethings build up our spiritual bank account and make us very rich in Heaven. Therefore, let's "count it all as joy" when the trials come, for we have to have some trial to overcome in order to become overcomers, in order for the works of God to be manifested in us, in order to receive God's Somethings, in order to become like gold in God's kingdom, in order to have gold for Jesus.

GOD SO LOVED

Picture by
Curtis

God Molds Us and Perfumes Us

Suffering Brings Purification and Sanctification

Suffering can become a purifying process that brings us closer to a holy God, providing we trust and love Him through His Son Jesus Christ and do not allow our trials to make us bitter. Sometimes in the midst of severe trials, we bitterly say, "God is doing so and so to me" and ask, "Why is this happening to me?" But the truth is that the enemy of our souls, the devil, brings troubles our way, and God sometimes allows it for our purification. But He gives grace to handle it. The thorns of life can only be borne with grace through the help of the spirit of God in us. Without the spirit, those thorns could make us bitter. In Ps. 119:92, the Psalmist states: *"Unless thy law had been my delights I should then have perished in mine affliction."* We have to continually ask for His grace and mercy to help us to go through, leaning on His strength all the time and delighting in His word.

So suffering should bring a purification, as is written in 2 Timothy 2:21: *"If a man therefore purge himself from these he shall be a vessel unto honor, sanctified, and meet for the master's use, and prepared unto every good work."* The Lord wants to make us golden vessels fit for God's use, people He can hold up before Satan's scrutiny and say, "Have you considered my servant?" "Consider my servant Joe," or "Consider my servant Joan," or whatever your name may be, just as He said to him, *"Have you considered my servant Job."*

27

Crucifying the Flesh for the Fellowship of His Sufferings

The flesh has to be crucified for the vessel to be molded perfectly. Crucifixion of self has to take place to bring us closer to God, until we can say, *"I am crucified with Christ,"* *"I live yet not I but Christ lives in me."* We have to learn to submit to God and to be completely yielded to the Holy Spirit for the flesh to be crucified.

Paul prayed, asking *"that I may know Him, and the power of His resurrection, and the fellowship of His sufferings, being made conformable unto His death."* And we also pray that we may know Him and the power of His resurrection, but we often leave out the rest of the verse. We do not want the fellowship of His sufferings. We do not want to wear the crown of thorns. But if we really want to be like our Lord and Saviour Jesus Christ, we must crucify the flesh. To receive His resurrection power, we must experience His sufferings too. We also must wear the crown of thorns. There is great significance in the crown of thorns and agape love, which comes with being made conformable to His sufferings. Only after we've suffered can we learn to love like Jesus. Only after we've suffered will all the pride and the ego leave. Only then will we decrease and Jesus increase within us.

Crown of Thorns and Sweet Fragrances

Crush the blossoms and the fragrance comes through. When the rose is crushed, the sweetness of the rose scent is captured. So we, as we're crushed by adversities and pricked by the thorns of affliction, can in time become like Jesus, with the sweetness of the agape love of Jesus outflowing from us as we learn to bear the fruit of patience, long-suffering, and kindness. For how can you know compassion until you've suffered awhile? [. . . *after that ye have suffered awhile, make you perfect* . . . (1 Pet. 5:10.)] And how can

28

you truly love unless you've learned to cry? "He washed my eyes with tears that I might see," as the song goes.

The enemy may put crowns of thorns upon our heads, but if we endure and obey God, those crowns of thorns will bring crowns of glory [. . . *ye shall receive a crown of glory that fadeth not away.* (1 Pet. 5:4.)] and we know that God is preparing to reward us with golden crowns for us to wear in Heaven. Endurance of the crowns of thorns will also bring the sweet fragrance of Jesus into our bodies and into our lives, the sweet-smelling Rose of Sharon, the hauntingly beautiful scent of the Lily of the Valley, and the awesome gifts of the Holy Spirit.

When one gains success with the favor on one's side after going through trouble, the world calls it coming out "smelling like a rose." As Christians, when we go through the trials and fires of life, and endure the crown of thorns, the Lord wants us to come out, not with the smell of ashes, but perfumed with the sweet essence of Jesus upon our beings; for Jesus is with us in the fire and the Balm of Gilead is always available to soothe the wounds from the crown of thorns. It's amazing how satan steals the things of God, for to really come out smelling like a rose is literally to smell like Jesus, the Rose of Sharon.

When we consider the beautiful and wonderful rewards that God has for us, the fruits of the spirit and the awesome gifts of the Holy Spirit, the sweet fragrances of his anointing, the beautiful heavenly crowns, we have to say of our troubles, "Lord, it's a very slim price to pay, indeed!" For *". . . eye hath not seen, nor ear heard, neither has entered into the heart of man, the things which God hath prepared for them that love him"* (1 Cor. 2:9). In Romans 8:18, it is written: *"For I reckon that the sufferings of this present time are not worthy to be compared with the glory which shall be revealed in us."*

There is a religious picture I've seen that says exactly what I've been trying to say about the crown of thorns and love. It's the "Sacred Heart" picture of Jesus, with the crown of thorns upon His head and His heart bleeding because of His great love for mankind. For me, the love of God really shines through that picture.

Let the Potter Do His Work

We have to allow the Potter to put us through the good and the bad, in order that we be made into His likeness and perfumed by His spirit. It's interesting what Job said in Job 2:10: *". . . Shall we receive good at the hand of God and shall we not receive evil? . . ."*

Sometimes when the persecution in the trials is very strong and the Master is using circumstances to chip away my pride and ego, I tend to think:

O God, I know I said I wanted to be like gold, even 24-karat gold in your Kingdom, but Lord, you know, right now, Lord, silver would do. I know I've said I want to be like you. I know I said I wanted to love like you. I know I said I wanted to be able to love those who do not love me, but O God, I need a rest now from all the persecution and troubles.

I tend to think like that when the fire gets very hot and I feel that I need a breather between fires, but then the Lord helps me to endure as He attempts to mold me into His vessel, letting me know that once He, the Potter, has started His work to make of me a golden vessel, He's not about to stop until He accomplishes His task. Praise God!

"If you have ever had a vision of God, you may try as you like to be satisfied on a lower level but God will never let you" (from *My Ultimate for His Highest,* Discovery House Publishers, n.d.).

God is not satisfied with anything less than perfection. He wants me to go all the way, **to go for the gold, and to bring this gold for Jesus!**

Trust God for His Best Gifts

I read in the *Daily Word*: "When we doubt God's goodness some of His best gifts—such as trials—will seem like bad gifts."

We have to trust God and know that He knows what is best for us in every situation and that He knows the outcome of every situation and that His way is best. He is the all-wise, all-powerful, all-knowing God, who loves us with an everlasting love and who will never, ever leave us or forsake us. I wish to share the following from my diary for Sunday, April 30, 1995:

Before I was fully awake the Lord had me singing or I should say the Holy Spirit sang to my heart and I found myself singing the song over and over again—a song I had heard on WFME. In my sleep-waking state I found myself singing the song as if I knew it by heart.

"God is too wise to be mistaken
God is too good to be unkind
So when you don't understand
When you don't see his plan
When you can't trace his hand
Trust His Heart"

In my sleep I sang it many times—singing it over and over again. When I awoke I realized the message the Lord had for me through the song. I had been to a service the night before at a church where the African evangelist, Teresia Warimu, was ministering. This evangelist being highly gifted in spiritual gifts has the gift of the Word of knowledge along with the working of miracles. Her habit during the services seems to be to pray for many people in the congregation and, being a small church, that night she prayed for mostly everyone. Yet she did not actually pray for me—at least not out loud. It seemed that every time she came to me, she stopped praying or asked one of her aides to pray—I couldn't understand why she wouldn't pray for me. She looked very kindly at me and even held my hand but never prayed for me, and I have to be honest with myself and say I was disappointed and a little hurt but deep down in my soul I knew God was in it. (I comforted myself by remembering that I receive a lot of prayer from my own church and have nothing to complain about.)

So when the Lord gave me that song, the next morning I was comforted. I thought that perhaps the Lord was saying that I need to be in the fire a little longer in order to learn to trust God and know that the fourth man is in the fire with me. I also thought that perhaps the Lord was saying that the feast that He is preparing is not yet fully cooked. He had brought the thought to my spirit some time ago that if I try to bring myself out of these trials ahead of His timing, it's like coming to a feast while the food is still undercooked, the meat still raw and the cake not risen and I would not enjoy the feast. In fact I would get a stomach ache! and perhaps much worse! Praise God for His love and understanding. Yes, Lord I will "Trust Your Heart" and allow the Potter to do His work in me—allow you to cook the meal to perfection.

[When I began to write this book I hoped it would not seem as though I was preaching, but now with all the scriptures jumping out at me (smile) as soon as I read the Word it seems I cannot help but preach the Word herein. So excuse me, my patient readers and friends, who read these thoughts which the Spirit has given me. I'm just excited about what God has to say to me on this subject matter.]

God is too good to be unkind. The trials He gives us are gifts to help us mature, and we shouldn't come out of these trials before these gifts themselves come to full maturity, because when we accept the gifts of trials He is able to give us the beautiful gift of His glory! Hallelujah! As the Word tells that these light afflictions work for us a far more exceeding and eternal weight of glory (2 Cor. 4:17). Just imagine, God gives us the light of His glory, the weight of which is so heavy that it lasts for all eternity, when we go through our troubles, which are described as *light* afflictions lasting only for a moment as compared to eternity! The Bible also says: ". . . when he is tried he shall receive the crown of life . . ." (James 1:12). You cannot receive the crown (a gift) unless you have been tried! Again it is written: "Every good gift . . . from the Father of lights . . ." (James 1:17). The trials of life are gifts which God gives us in order for us to receive His crown of glory—His crown of light upon us. This light is our inheritance as Christians (Eph. 1:18). And did not Jesus our Lord say in His great high priestly prayer: ". . . the glory thou hast given me I have given unto them"? Yes, this glory, this crown of light is our inheritance as children of God. But we can only receive this inheritance when we trust God and yield to the gift of trials!

Running for the Gold

One Sunday evening after I got home, I laughed at myself while writing the following paragraphs regarding victories I had received that day:

While sitting in church this morning, I couldn't help but think how great the trials the past week had been and the fire was very hot. And during the message, the Holy Spirit was chastising me as well as encouraging me and like a father with a small child—scolding and then petting; and I went from tears to laughter, and the Lord made me look up at the ceiling and see the brass around the rims of the lights shining like gold and reminded me that I'm supposed to be **in the running for the gold** and it wasn't supposed to be easy.

The Holy Spirit ended the service giving us three beautiful messages in tongues with interpretations that His presence was with us and that His presence brings joy, taking away all the insecurities and fears. All three prophecies were about His light and His presence. And I felt the Lord was speaking to me personally, especially concerning His light because He knows I like to bask in the light when His presence comes upon me. I just like to stand still in His glory light and bask in His presence when that light manifests, forgetting all my problems while God just washes them away with His light. God is wonderful, I know! How can I ever complain? He makes all things work for my good anyway! Then, of course, as the service ended, that beautiful blanket of light came down from Heaven and made me feel wonderful. I managed to resist the devil and the temptation to speak out of turn to someone concerning something that was on my mind, and I left the service with victory in my spirit and love in my heart.

However, I fell when I got to Mom's when she offered me dinner and I said, yes, eagerly looking forward to eating it, even though I had made a new promise to fast forty days and this was only the second day; so I ate the dinner (one of my favorites, scobeach fish and rice with red beans) knowing that the next day I would have to start my covenant all over again, remembering with fear and trepidation that it is written *"When you vow a vow unto God differ not to pay it."* Lord help me!

Thank God for His patience with me! Sometimes it seems that not one day can go by without my giving in to the devil in one way or another. However, I felt good that I didn't give in regarding the temptation to speak out of turn to someone concerning something that was on my mind and that I was able to leave the service with victory in my spirit. I received deliverance in the service even though it may not have been all the deliverance I wanted, but I received deliverance, I know, in my spirit and rejoiced in that. Help me, Lord, to wait on you so that you can make me twenty-four-karat gold. Even as I write "twenty-four-karat gold," I wince in my spirit, knowing that it hurts a lot to run for twenty-four-karat gold in the Kingdom of God. But, Lord, I know if I trust you, you will make the running easy. Praise your Holy Name.

I have to remember that twenty-four-karat gold requires a lot of rejoicing in the face of extreme difficulties. For it is written, *"In everything give thanks, for this is the will of God in Christ Jesus concerning you."* Tonight we sang and repeated several times, "Nothing is too difficult for God." I am the Lord the God of all flesh

and nothing is too hard for me. Is there anything too hard for God?
Nothing is too hard for God.

Hallelujah!!!!!! Amen.

GOD SO LOVED

Picture by
Curtis

God Encourages Us to Bear the Fruit of the Spirit

Cultivate Fruit—No Law against Such

It is written in Gal. 5:22–23: *"But the fruit of the Spirit is love, joy, peace, long-suffering, gentleness, goodness, faith, meekness, temperance: against such there is no law."*

I consider the fruit of the spirit of God and the love of God too deep and great subjects to speak about fully in a small book such as this. They would need to be expounded upon by a far greater student of the holy scriptures than myself. However, the following are some thoughts that I'd like to express concerning growing and cultivating the love of God as it relates to our running for the spiritual gold in our pilgrimage through this life. We are instructed in Galatians to bear the fruit of the spirit, which is love, joy, peace, long-suffering, gentleness, goodness, faith, meekness, and temperance.

We really have no choice but to cultivate and bear fruit if we want to obtain the gold medal for Jesus. Running the race to obtain the spiritual gold helps us to cultivate and grow the best and sweetest kind of the fruit of the spirit in our lives.

When the worst of times brings out the best in people, we call it bearing the fruit of the spirit. It is at such times that the best fruit can be cultivated if we yield our lives to God's will. When our response to hatred is love, to gloom and fear is joy and faith, to catastrophe is peace, it is then that our human spirit is becoming

37

Christlike and that is what Paul means when he says, *". . . against such there is no law."*

To really have all the fruit of the spirit manifesting in one's life is a very difficult thing to do for the natural man. This requires a person to be a saint, and no less! But then, that's what God says we are, saints! If you really have love, joy, peace, long-suffering, gentleness, goodness, faith, meekness, and temperance, then you are truly walking the highway of holiness and on the way to Heaven where you can't be turned back. No wonder Paul says, *"against such there is no law"!* No law can come against you.

Love—the Root of the Fruit

Paul goes on to say in Rom. 8:35–39:

Who shall separate us from the love of Christ? Shall tribulation, or distress, or persecution, or famine, or nakedness, or peril, or sword? As it is written, For thy sake we are killed all the day long; we are accounted as sheep for the slaughter. Nay, in all these things we are more than conquerors through Him that love us. For I am persuaded, that neither death, nor life, nor angels, nor principalities, nor powers nor things present, nor things to come, nor height, nor depth, nor any other creature, shall be able to separate us from the love of God, which is in Christ Jesus our Lord.

I mean, if we really have all the beautiful qualities of the fruit of the spirit in our spirit and character, who or what can defeat us! Nothing can separate us from the love of God! And actually, although there are nine parts of the fruit of the spirit, only one part is needed for the others to grow—and that is the fruit of love. Love is the foundation and base of the fruit of the spirit. All the other parts of the fruit spring and grow from love. None of the other fruit can grow fully and completely without love. As it is written in 1

Corinthians 13, without love we are nothing in our Christian lives and walk with God. Without love the manifestation of joy, peace, faith, goodness, etc., manifests as hypocrisy! Love has to be the root of the fruit! Love has to be the foundation and base of all that we do. Love does not lack for joy and peace. If you don't have God's divine love indwelling, you certainly can't be long-suffering for very long. Love is full of gentleness, goodness and meekness. Love is what feeds faith. Gal. 5:6 tells us that faith works by love. The strength of love is needed for self-control to manifest.

In Col. 3:12–14, it is written: *"Put on therefore, as the elect of God, holy and beloved, bowels of mercies, kindness, humbleness of mind, meekness, long-suffering; Forbearing one another, and forgiving one another, if any man have a quarrel against any: even as Christ forgave you, so also do ye. And above all these things put on love, which is the bond of perfectness."*

This is no small order the Lord gives us in the above scriptures. But God helps us by His Holy Spirit, to put on bowels of mercies even in our times of distress. For the child of God, the fruit of the spirit grows with more quality and depth when it is challenged to grow, during times of adversities and during distressing circumstances and in an atmosphere of hardships, difficulties, and trials and when one is put to the test, is forced to overcome temptations and hazardous circumstances by doing good and allowing God's spirit to triumph over evil, by allowing Jesus to be Lord over one's life in difficult times.

Some people may argue this point and say how can something so lovely as the fruit of love, peace, and joy grow in adverse circumstances when the enemy is battering us with negative emotions and stressful spirits. But the truth is that if you are expressing love, peace, joy, long-suffering, faith, goodness in the happy times, it is not necessarily a love, peace, joy, long-suffering, faith, and goodness of any depth. Surface love, peace, joy, long-suffering, faith and goodness can flourish in happy and sunshiny times. However, deep, true, and lasting love, peace, joy, long-suffering, faith, and goodness come after they have been tested by the rains of adversities, the winds of distressing circumstances, and the storms of uncertain times.

Love—the Sweet Fruit

Like physical fruit, spiritual fruit has to have a certain amount of rain and sunshine to grow. Therefore, even as it takes the rain to make the flowers grow, so the rains of adversity soften and prepare our hearts for the fruit of love to grow. Fruit also needs the warmth of sunshine to ripen. Green fruit is not good to eat. As a child, I was told not to eat the green fruit off the tree or it would hurt my stomach. Bitter fruit is not good for anybody to eat. The fruit of the spirit is defiled by bitterness. The fruit must be ripe and sweet. So the fruit of love needs the warmth of God's spirit in our hearts to ripen sufficiently so that it's edible to the Lord's taste, when he wants to use us to minister to others—that we may minister with love. When we are literally baptized in God's great love, we can say that the sunshine of God's spirit has warmed our hearts and the fruit of love is growing in our hearts whereby we can yield to His desires for our lives. Let the fruit of our spirits be sweet to the taste of all who eat it, and let us become the apple of His eye. **The gold of the fruit of the spirit of love is the present Jesus wants us to bring to Him when He tells us to buy gold tried in the fire.**

In 1 Corinthians 13, it is written:

Though I speak with the tongues of men and of angels, and have not love, I am become as sounding brass, or a tinkling cymbal. And though I have the gift of prophecy, and understand all mysteries, and all knowledge; and though I have all faith, so that I could remove mountains, and have not love, I am nothing. And though I bestow all my goods to feed the poor, and though I give my body to be burned, and have not love, it profiteth me nothing. Love suffereth

*long, and is kind; love envieth not; love vaunteth not itself, is not
puffed up, doth not behave itself unseemly, seeketh not her own, is
not easily provoked, thinketh no evil; rejoiceth not in iniquity, but
rejoiceth in the truth; beareth all things, believeth all things, hopeth
all things, endureth all things. Love never faileth. . . .*

In my church, the Holy Spirit ministers deliverance from evil
spirits and the fruit of love has to be evident in one's life if one is
to become a deliverance worker, or "demon chaser," as we say
sometimes. I sometimes notice a certain sister as she prays for
others. How broken her spirit becomes as she prays and how she
cries for the person as she prays and I have to say, "Lord, I don't
have the love this sister has. She cries for people. She feels what
they feel. The love is obvious in her. I feel like a hypocrite beside
her."

I've asked the Lord to help me bear the fruit of love, and I see
that after I pray this way, certain situations develop in my life and
bring difficult people and trying circumstances into my life. And I
realize that after I pray this way for love to be manifested in me that
the Lord has to break me as the potter does the clay and mold me
anew to the Spirit's specifications as I surrender my will to His, as
I decrease and allow Jesus to increase in me, as I allow Jesus to be
Lord of my life.

Gal. 5:24–25 says: *"And they that are Christ's have crucified
the flesh with the affections and lusts. If we live in the Spirit, let us
also walk in the Spirit."*

The Softening of the Heart to Love

Even as I write this "love chapter" for this book, I've noticed
certain new circumstances involving showing love to difficult people have cropped up in my everyday life. The Lord is saying to me
if I'm to write about His love I must practice it. He has to humble

41

me in some way as the potter does his work to make me more like Jesus, so that I can love like Jesus loves. He has to soften me. As it is written in Job 23:16: *"For God maketh my heart soft and the Almighty troubleth me."* And there is a song that goes like this:

He washed my eyes with tears that I might see
He tore it all apart and looked inside
He found it filled with fears and foolish pride
He swept away the things that made me blind
And then I saw the clouds were silver-lined
And now I understand 'twas best for me
He washed my eyes with tears that I might see
And now I'm glad he came so tenderly
And washed my eyes with tears that I might see

When the Spirit of the Lord softens our hearts with tears as we intercede for others and we are touched by the infirmities and needs of those we're interceding for, and we become broken before God, it is then that the sunshine of God's love can warm our hearts with God's agape. This breaking of our spirits, this complete yielding to God, this brokenness before God—whether the brokenness comes through intercessory prayer or through the utter realization of our smallness and filthiness before a great and holy God as His anointing touches our hearts, or simply through some distressing situation—can be the start of the softening of our hearts, to accept and hold God's mighty love within our mortal souls.

One very rarely sees a person who truly has the fruit of love in their lives acting like "Mr. Know-It-All" and full of pride. This spirit of love comes through suffering. People who truly love are humble and gentle and have been softened by tears, have suffered in some way, have gone through the refiner's fire; and have been molded by the Master Potter's hands. In such people, the spirit of humility, a strong gentleness and quiet assurance, accompanies the spirit of love and to such people we can say, "I see Jesus in you."

That's why I say that if one has the fruit of love, one also has to have all the other parts of the fruit—joy, peace, long-suffering, gentleness, goodness, faith, meekness, and temperance, because love is the basis of all joy, peace, long-suffering, gentleness, goodness, faith, meekness, and temperance. People with the true love of God have been softened by tears. I hear my pastor say, "Be broken before God." I realize he means to be repentant and humble before God. But I also see another softening of the heart by the tears that flow through affliction and sorrow and suffering. That's why the song says, "He washed my eyes with tears that I might see. . . . He swept away the things that made me blind. . . ."

Therefore we consider love—and we're talking about agape love, divine love—the love that asks for nothing in return. We can love our families and friends and those who show us favor because it's easy for the human nature to love when we are loved. But to love those who do not love us or to even just show favor and pray for those we consider our enemies is a most difficult thing to do and can only be done successfully by and through the Holy Spirit living in us and having a keen desire to please God.

Forgiveness in Love

So I've come to realize that the love of God does not manifest in our spirits until we've been tested and tried; for how can we say we love if we cannot forgive? How can I pray for others and feel what they feel in their trials if I haven't experienced testings and trials myself? How can I experience the fruit of love if I haven't forgiven? The Lord entreats us and begs us to love one another. He does not want us in unforgiveness and strife. He wants the Body of Christ in unity and harmony. If we fight, we destroy each other. If we love, we build the Body of Christ. Only love can make the Body whole. Only love can make the Body grow. Only love can heal the Body. Only love can make the Body work. It is written in 1 John

4:12: "... *If we love one another God dwelleth in us and His love is perfected in us.*"

Jesus speaks of the importance of forgiveness many times. In Luke 17:1–4, Jesus speaks of forgiving our brothers and how terrible a thing it is for one of His children to be offended and what a horrible thing would happen to those who offend His children. As I read this scripture again, I am impressed in my spirit as to the importance of reading all the verses connected to what Jesus is saying here and not just the first verse. So many times just one verse of a subject is read or quoted and the complete revelation is missed. The words of Jesus should be read carefully because one verse of His words is often directly connected to the previous verse or the following verse, and if we don't read carefully, the true and full revelation of what He's saying can be lost to us. That's why scripture should not be taken out of context but the whole subject of which He is speaking should be studied. An example of the connection of Jesus' words rings in these words of our Lord about offense and unforgiveness:

> *Then said he unto the disciples, It is impossible but that offenses will come: but woe unto him, through whom they come! It were better for him that a millstone were hanged about his neck, and he cast into the sea, than that he should offend one of these little ones. Take heed to yourselves: If thy brother trespass against thee, rebuke him; and if he repent, forgive him. And if he trespass against thee seven times in a day, and seven times in a day turn again to thee, saying I repent; thou shalt forgive him.*

> —Luke 17: 1–4

When we read Luke 17:1 and 2, which tells us that offenses will come but woe unto he who brings the offenses, we also have to read verses 3 and 4, which speak of forgiveness. And verses 3 and 4 are saying that although offenses come, we must be quick to forgive the offender. We must remember that Jesus was not speaking to heathens but to believers and people considered as children of God. He says if thy *brother* trespass against thee, forgive him. Here we see the Holy Spirit speaking to Christians and telling us that we should quickly forgive one another as children of God because when we offend each other, we risk putting a great burden of judgment on each other. We can put millstones around each other's necks and hang each other and put each other in the sea, as is written in Luke 17:2, if we lay blame on each other and not only offend by our unforgiveness but risk the judgment of God upon ourselves for being unforgiving.

Also, through unforgiveness, we are fighting each other instead of fighting the devil, who is the real cause of the problem, for we wrestle not against flesh and blood but against principalities and the rulers of the darkness of this world. By being unforgiving toward our own brothers and sisters, who have the Holy Spirit indwelling in them, we bring the curse of God upon our own lives. In Gal. 5;15, Paul says: *"But if ye bite and devour one another, take heed that ye be not consumed one of another."* The Lord stresses forgiveness in other parts of the gospel in which he says to *forgive seventy times* and he is actually saying, *forgive—always forgive your brother and sister*.

We can only say we love God if we love each other. Saint John said: *". . . for he that loveth not his brother whom he hath seen, how can he love God whom he hath not seen?"* Love for God must gloriously overshadow everything that we do and say and think, and God will be with us every step of the way. We must know that God is with us every step of the way in all our trials. We are the prize that Jesus, the real gold medal champion, won for the Father. We must know that we are worth a lot to God, for He gave His Son for us. We must know that we are priceless and precious to God. In Isa. 43:4, the Holy Spirit says: *"Since thou wast precious in my sight, thou hast been honorable, and I have loved thee: therefore will I give men for thee, and people for thy life."*

Loving like Jesus

In the Body of Christ many people are going through many trials, and I think that God's aim in all our various trials is to bring us to a real spirit of agape love, a love that loves without wanting anything in return, without conditions, that loves like Jesus loves.

In the Fellowship, for now we have been whittled down to a very few compared to the large numbers we used to be and God continues to stress in all the messages love and sincerity. It seems that God is allowing us to see each others' bad points, as well as our good points, in order to test our love for one another, in order to help us to love unconditionally, for how can you say you love someone if you've never had to react to their negative side. The thought comes to me that if we love, we have to love the person as they really are and not just for their "Sunday" appearance. As for myself, in my sixteen to seventeen years at the Fellowship, it's been only lately that I've gotten to know some people in the ministry well enough to see their negative sides, their weekday sides so to speak, the side that one sees when a person relaxes and "lets their hair down." Yes, it seems that God is bringing us into situations where we see each other's Monday-through-Saturday sides as well as our Sunday side. God wants us to love the person when we see them in a harassed, worried, confused, angry, and even downright nasty state as well as when we see them on Sunday in the midst of the anointing as loving, sweet, kind, compassionate human beings who are at total peace with themselves and with God. If we can love the person in all their ways Sunday through Saturday, then we can say we love the whole person and not just a part of them. But how can we say we love if it's only for their Sunday side? Do we love only on Sunday and never on Monday, Tuesday, Wednesday, Thursday, Friday, or Saturday? I believe God wants us to see the good and the bad in each other so that we can learn to love unconditionally, and also so that we will see each other as normal people who sometimes make mistakes and not as supersaints whose feet never

46

touch this earth. I believe God wants us to love each other as Jesus loves us, in spite of all our faults.

When we see each other as we really are, we will worship only Him and not each other! I know there was a time when I thought most of the congregation were better saints than myself and I sort of secretly hero-worshipped some saints and thought I would aspire to be like certain people whom I admired for their spirituality. This in itself is not a bad thing to do if the person admired is like Jesus, and Jesus Himself may well point to another saint when we ask Him, "Let me see you"! Of course, as I grew in the Lord, my aim became to be like Jesus and look at only Him, and I learned to take my eyes from people and to look at Jesus, the one who loves me with all my faults, the one who loves with an everlasting love. I would like to love like Jesus loves. I have a long way to go!!

The Test of Our Love for God

All our testings, trials, and tribulations in this life are the real test of the love of God in us, the test of the degree of the love of God in us, and the test of our love for God. The way in which we react to all our trials shows the degree of our love for God. It is written in Col. 1:10: *"Walk worthy of the Lord unto all pleasing, being fruitful in every good work, and increasing in the knowledge of God."*

Love is the gold we must bring to Jesus.

47

GOD SO
LOVED

Picture by
Curtis

God Encourages Us to Rejoice and Praise Him

Learning to Be Thankful

God yearns for our thanks and allows situations to come into our daily lives that will lead us to thank Him. God commands us to give thanks, and He knows that when we give thanks, we'll gain joy and it will be easier to rejoice. Jesus tells of the woman who lost the piece of silver and when she found it rejoiced greatly, calling her neighbors and asking them to rejoice with her, for she had found the piece of silver that she'd lost (Luke 15:9).

I experience situations in my life from time to time when something happens to bring me agitation and dismay, and then the Lord performs a miracle or sends someone to speak to me that is like a message from God, the effect of which is like a light turned on in a dark room. Then I become so joyful and thankful all I can do is rejoice and praise Him and say, "Thank you Jesus, for loving me so much," especially when it's obviously a miracle.

There was the time when I couldn't find my keys to my apartment in the midst of a very busy schedule and already trying circumstances because the car was acting up. If I turned it off, it wouldn't start because of battery trouble and I'd have to get a jumpstart. I had been making a few trips from my car to the apartment, carrying things back and forth. As I hurried the second time up to my apartment from the car, I asked the Lord to send an angel to show me where the keys were because I realized that I'd left my keys in the apartment after the first trip, but I couldn't remember where. I'd left the car on to keep the battery going.

As I came into the apartment, I didn't know where to look first and then the miracle happened. I heard a noise from the kitchen sink as if one plate knocked against another. When I looked by the sink, there were the keys on the kitchen cabinet. I was so overjoyed all I could do was raise my hands and give thanks as the kitchen cabinet became my altar to God for a minute or two. As soon as I asked for the assistance of the angels, God had an angel literally direct me by the sound in the kitchen sink to where the keys were. They could have been anywhere in the apartment, and I would have spent a lot of time looking in the bathroom, bedroom, living room, dining area, etc., before I looked in the kitchen because the kitchen would have been the last place I would have looked. But that's how God takes care of us and sends angels to assist us. *"For are they not all ministering spirits sent to minister unto the heirs of salvation"* (Heb. 1:14). Praise the Lord! Thank the Lord!

I remember my pastor telling us once to make a list of the miracles God performs in our lives each day—to keep a note-book—and I see why he told us to do that. Because when we realize that every day God performs miracles for us, it builds our faith and brings much joy to one's spirit and we maintain a spirit of thankfulness.

Learning to Pray

When suffering bring us closer to God, we learn to pray and praise as never before, reaching higher heights and deeper depths, for nothing can make us concentrate on God when in prayer more than when despair and great longing are knocking us down on our knees to touch Almighty God to see and hear with our problem.

When the Lord allowed the enemy to seemingly surround me with certain trials in the fires of life, I was amazed at how I could stay all day in prayer, once praying for at least ten hours, praising and worshipping God. When my son went to work that morning, I was on my knees and when he came home that night, I was still worshipping God. Without this great need and desire for deliverance, I may not have been so diligent in keeping this covenant to pray all day. But one of the ministers at church had suggested this covenant of a whole day of praise to God and I, being in great need, kept this covenant, for at this time nothing was more important to me than hearing from God and pleasing God. *"My soul longeth for thee in a dry and thirsty land. . . ."*

Sometimes in great suffering we just want to stay under the shelter of the Most High, and it's at such times that He really becomes our greatest and best friend. When talking about the problem doesn't help, or there's no one to talk to, we can just stay talking to Jesus. The world may say we've gone into a shell or become introspective, but the truth is that He's hiding us and sheltering us in the cleft of the rock, the rock Christ Jesus. Some may call it being on the backside of the mountain, or just being in a desert place, a wilderness, but it's in this place that we learn to pray, grow close to God, and receive the most wonderful gift of His anointing, His presence upon our lives. Praise the Lord God Almighty! And thank God for hearing and answering our prayers.

Let's sing to the Lord:

In the trial I find a blessing
In the fire I see His face
Oh, the glory that surrounds me
>   *Since the Saviour walks with me.*

Learning to Rejoice

In Hannah Hurnard's book *Hind's Feet on High Places,* the character Much Afraid's name is later changed to Grace and Glory, and her companions, Suffering and Sorrow, changed to Joy and Peace. So our companions of suffering and sorrow can later be turned into grace, glory, joy, and peace if we walk the narrow path God wants us to take and learn to rejoice and praise God in the trying circumstances of our lives and not take the broad and commonly treaded path of bitterness.

To rejoice in the face of utmost trials is one of the most difficult things to do. To "grin and bear it," as the British say, to put on a happy front, to laugh when you want to cry. But that's what God wants the child of God to do. That's one of the ways we become more like Jesus, by rejoicing during our own difficulties and praying for someone else who is in trouble; and that can only be done by the spirit of God working in us.

Why rejoice? Paul says to *"rejoice for your redemption draweth nigh"* and *"rejoice evermore."* Jesus says to *"rejoice and be glad because great is your reward in heaven"* and also, *"rejoice because our names are written down in the Lamb's book of life."*

If we don't rejoice, the door to our spirit is left ajar for the terrible two (Doom and Gloom) who are waiting to burst the door wide open to come in with their brother Fear who brings with him all sorts of other evil spirits who take away the victory. So we must bind the strongmen of Gloom, Doom, and Fear and loosen Joy upon ourselves by rejoicing evermore.

The following is an insert from my diary during a very distressing time in my life:

God gives me songs in my night. Lately I've noticed that in spite of the turmoil and the dark storms, a song comes to me as if in answer to my thoughts, queries, and reveries. I find myself humming a song inwardly and if I hum it out, it brings a certain kind of sweet joy and peace that only comes from the Holy Spirit. It's as if my Heavenly Father is speaking to me in song. It's as if He's encouraging me. (And I thought the Lord wasn't speaking to me anymore. But He speaks in different ways.)

Do not the Psalms speak of singing aloud unto God who is our strength and making a joyful noise unto the Lord! And does not the joy of the Lord become our strength as we practice the joy! God wants me to sing His praises. I noticed this morning how the praises flowed from me in tongues as a song. God wants me to sing to Him. I will sing unto the Lord, for He has triumphed gloriously. I will sing unto the Lord! For so long now He's been saying to me one word, "Rejoice!," and I remember how I saw the word "PRAISE," in lights across the altar. Many times that was all He would say.

Lately, in the last couple of years, in what I consider to be a night season of my life, it seems He's not saying anything. But now He's giving me songs. Jesus always helps us to do what He wants us to do. He gives a helping hand with what we find so difficult to achieve. He makes a way. Thank you, Jesus, for giving me grace to rejoice in my night. His grace is sufficient! He gives songs in the night. I will sing unto the Lord! Thank you, Jesus!

I remember once, while going through a thorny pathway, my spirit being very gloomy and sad, and I hardly able to sing to the Lord, the Holy Spirit said to me, "Be a Miriam." I knew He meant I should dance to the Lord. At my church we're frequently anointed at the altar, and at the next anointings, after the Lord told me to be a Miriam, I found my feet danced naturally in the spirit whenever I was anointed. It was after that also that I noticed the Holy Spirit directed my pastor to have sisters, who were going through deep trials, to dance to Jesus at the altar. God is so good. He always helps us to do what we find most difficult, and if He tells you to do something, He makes a way to do that thing. He shows us off to the enemy: "Have you considered my servant!"

God's Servants

To become God's servants, priests, and kings unto God, we have to rejoice while we're being purified, tested, and tried. Then we can say, *"The King shall joy in thy strength, O Lord, and in thy salvation how greatly shall He rejoice! Thou hast given him his heart's desire, and has not withholden the request of his lips. For thou presentest him with the blessings of goodness: thou settest a crown of pure gold on his head"* (Ps. 21:1–3). Hallelujah!

The enemy of our souls, the devil, may want to call us bad names, keep us down, and even have us thinking badly of ourselves, but God calls us His servants, His priests, His kings and His queens and His princesses, His beloved children. And thank God that He doesn't see us with our mistakes, but He sees us wearing golden crowns, as His rejoicing servants, kings, and priests unto Him.

The Darker the Night, the Brighter the Stars Shine

There is a song that goes like this:

> *The darker the night*
> *The brighter the light shines*
> *I'm walking with Jesus*
> *The light of the world*
> *For He is my light*
> *In Him there's no darkness*
> *The darker the night*
> *The brighter the light*
> *When I walk with Him*

We should go through our trials and tests, rejoicing and skipping, like little children, but most often we're crying and limping. When we're going through a dark time in our lives and we go through rejoicing and skipping, our star shines brightly in the Shekinah of God. For He loves it when we rejoice and skip along life's rough pathways, like children without a care, holding onto His hand.

The song says, "The darker the night, the brighter the *Light* shines," and I say, "The darker the night, the brighter the *Stars* shine," for we children of God are as stars in a dark world and our stars must always shine brightly. I'm becoming more and more determined that "this light of mine, I'm gonna make it shine," no matter what the devil does. The Lord commands us, *"Rejoice, and again I say, Rejoice!"* God's will is for us to rejoice!

The Light and the Junk

During adverse times we may find the negative side of our personalities being exposed and may well ask, how can darkness and light live together? As for myself, I think about various situations in my life that I call my trials, the various things happening that cause me to fret and that bring the darkness. Yet I know the glory of God is with me. I see His light upon me! Yet how can all the anger and the unforgiveness still manifest! We have the light but there are still areas of darkness in our personalities which show up in times of stress and suffering, which if not cast out can cause trouble in our spiritual life, and growth in the Lord can be hindered. These areas of darkness can be as the thorns that spring up and choke the Word. These areas of darkness are often the "hidden" dirt in our lives, the sides we don't want anyone to see. These areas of darkness can cause the light to dim or to go away, leaving us in entire darkness, and God may ask, "Where is thy beautiful flock?" (Jer. 13:20: "**. . . where is the flock that was given thee, thy beautiful flock?**") Yes, indeed, God's flock of light around us may depart with the growth of the dark junk.

These areas of darkness, these blotches in our personalities, which we may call "the junk" in our spirit—like unforgiveness, jealousy, envy, greed, various kinds of lust and fears of all kinds—do not all automatically leave when we receive Christ. The light we receive from the anointing of the glory that God gives us

55

at salvation and which comes with the baptism of the Holy Spirit helps us to deal with this junk in our spirit and squash it to a degree, but the junk needs to be cast out or it keeps popping up like weeds in a garden. The junk is evil spirits, which plague our walk in the Lord. The junk is like the dross, which leaves the gold as the gold is purified. The junk is like that which falls off the diamond as the diamond is cleansed. I guess we could also say that the junk is the ego and that's why we need to let the ego decrease with all its proud manifestations and let God's spirit within us increase and fill us fully. (Eph. 3:19: **"And to know the love of Christ which passeth all knowledge that ye might be filled with all the fullness of Christ."**)

These perverse spirits, such as envy, greed, lust, worries, fears, etc., are evil spirits in the personality that need to be cast out, and this can only be done by the power of God's Holy Spirit. The Holy Spirit casts out the junk through deliverance and by leading us into situations that crucify the flesh and decrease the junk. This decreasing of the junk comes only through adversity, which causes suffering and brings the light of self-examination, and in this self-examination that the Holy Spirit brings, the junk is exposed by the light of He the Holy Spirit and is then readily cast out.

Yes, while deliverance is one way the junk can leave, in order for these blotches in our personalities to stay away from us, God allows us to be put through Job-like situations to "crucify the flesh." When we go through these crucifying situations where we find ourselves crying out to God for deliverance, we often fast and pray and we need desperately to fast and pray because radical crucifixion of self comes only through yielding to a spirit of self-sacrificing to God. Only then in this seeking after sanctification will the light shine brighter within us, completely obliterating the darkness and the junk so that we will be as His jewels of diamonds and gold. Then we can become more Christlike, more like Him, shining brightly as the Bride of Christ should be, without spot or wrinkle or any such thing! Then we can say, as David said in Psalms 45:13:

"The King's daughter is all glorious within; her clothing is of wrought gold." This glorious light within is what Jesus wants to see in us. The King of glory wants to come in and live within us. **This light is the gold we must bring to Jesus.**

GOD SO LOVED

Picture by
Curtis

God Encourages Us to Be Useful

Encouragements As We Wrestle against the Powers of Darkness

Something to remember is that our condition can always worsen before it gets better, and if we could see into the spirit world, we would see God's angels fighting the demonic world on our behalf because someone prays for us, or just simply because God loves us and sees that we wouldn't be able to survive the fresh onslaught of evil that the devil's angels try to bring our way. As Jesus Christ said, *"The devil comes to steal, to kill and to destroy but I am come that they may have life and have it more abundantly."* Yes, even in the midst of trying circumstances, the devil sends new evil our way. But if we walk with God, the angels of God outnumber the devil's angels, and *"More are they that are for us than they that are against us."*

At the height of Daniel's fast, there was a tremendous battle being wrought in the heavens between the forces of evil and God's angels (Daniel 10). But God's angels were victorious over the powers of darkness, and Daniel got the victory. We wrestle not against flesh and blood but against principalities and powers and the rulers of the darkness of this world, as Paul tells us in the sixth chapter of Ephesians.

It's Only a Test

When we're going through our testing experiences, we can take heart in knowing that it's only a test, which will soon end. I am reminded of the radio announcer's voice, after the high-pitched signal and then silence, telling the public: "It's only a test. If it had been the real thing, you would have been instructed to do so and so." When the children of Israel sinned in the wilderness, their punishment was great. Some of them were swallowed up by the earth. In great contrast, the Blood of Jesus waits to forgive us with infinite mercy, when we turn back to God. *"It is of the Lord's mercies that we are not consumed, because His compassions fail not"* (Lam. 3:22).

In our times of distress, we don't have to worry that it's more than just a test or that it's something that will swallow us up, although some trials are so severe, we feel that it's doing just that. But we can be comforted that it is only a test, which will soon pass. We should not always think in the terms of punishment, that we're being punished. As born-again, forgiven Christians, we're not being punished. We're being tested. We can say to ourselves, "It's only a test and this too I shall overcome. It's only a test and I shall go on to higher heights and deeper depths in Christ Jesus." Thanks be unto God who always gives us the victory.

Resting Places

The Lord once showed me a vision of various fires. But in between the flames, there were things like slabs of flat rocks. After pondering on this, I realized that God was showing me a meaningful vision concerning my life, but I wasn't sure I liked it. However, as the next few years passed with some very hot fires, I realized that the Lord had showed me that there would be several fires but also that there would be resting places in between those fires. Just as

Jesus is our refuge in the storms, God provides resting places in between the trials. So the Lord wanted me to know that although there would be trials, He would provide refuge in the midst of the trials. Praise His Holy Name. Thank God that He helps us to endure, that He doesn't just leave us to struggle through, but that He is always there, providing a refuge when things get too tough, waiting to create a table in our wilderness, for He said, *"I will never leave thee nor forsake thee."*

To Become Useful in His Hands

Once, someone said, "If you are going to be used of God, He will take you through a multitude of experiences that are not necessarily meant for you. They are meant to make you useful in His hands." Joseph's brothers sold him into slavery, and he later became the second most important person in Egypt and the person to deliver his family in the time of famine and keep the tribe of Israel from dying out. After many years, when he saw them again, when they came to him seeking food in a foreign land, he said to them, *"You meant it for evil but God meant it unto good"* (Gen. 50:20). Sometimes we have to experience a certain type of suffering in order to be used by God. 2 Corinthians 1:4: *"Who comforteth us in all our tribulations, that we may be able to comfort them which are in any trouble, by the comfort wherewith we ourselves are comforted."*

Later You Will Know

The Lord once gave me these words—I don't remember if He spoke them or if I heard someone say them, but they made a great impression on my spirit: "You do not understand now what I do, but later you will know." In the King James version, the Word says:

"What I do thou knowest not now, but thou shall know hereafter" (John 13:7).

When we come to the place of deliverance and what God has for us, we can say, "Thank you, Lord, for this great reward and thank you, Lord, for taking me through. Indeed, Lord, it was a very slim price to pay." We begin to realize that God allows hardships into our lives so that we can become overcomers and be molded into golden vessels that He can pour His spirit into, vessels that He can use. We come to know that God allows us to go through persecutions so that we'll learn to obey Him and bear the fruit of the spirit, as written in Galatians 5, and that God allows the buffeting winds of adversity to rock our boats so that we'll learn to look to Him and to trust Him.

Two sisters in the Lord were having a conversation and one said to the other, "When this is over, my enemies will know who God is."

The other sister answered her wisely, saying, "When this is over, *you* will know who God is!"

God allows us to go through trying times so that we'll come to know fully who He is; that He is:

I AM that I AM—that He is:
Jehovah Jirah—that He is:
Redeemer of Israel and Saviour of the World—that He is:
The Bright and the Morning Star—that He is:
The Rose of Sharon and The Lily of the Valley—that He is:
King of Kings and Lord of Lords—that He is:
Jesus Christ the Son of the Living God—that He is:
The Great Physician—that He is:
The Healer of Galilee and the Balm of Gilead—that He is:
Almighty and Everlasting Father

Yes, later we come to understand and to realize that God indeed is very faithful and that every rough path He causes us to take is for our ultimate good, for *"All things work together for good to those who love the Lord to them who are the called according to His purpose"* (Rom. 8:28).

"Lord, prepare me to be your sanctuary, pure and holy, tried and true." Yes, God says, later you will know.

GOD SO LOVED

Picture by
Curtis

God Rewards Us

As a Result of the Trial

The Lord caused me to realize that victory can come to our spirits and added strength of purpose to go through, when we look at the blessing coming as a result of the trial that we're in. The Holy Spirit once said to me, "Your greatest trial, your biggest blessing." In other words, were it not for this trial, there would be no such blessing. The blessing may be spiritual, physical, or financial. But the blessing can only be received "as a result of" this present trial. Joseph's family were fed in famine as a result of the trials and persecutions he experienced.

While going through a very grueling college course, encouragement can come when one looks at one's future in the marketplace with a degree, rather than without a college education, when we see ourselves in the desired position. So trials can be like sitting for an examination that if we pass will bring good things into our lives.

The Lord said to Joshua, *"See, I have given you the victory."* We have to *see* the blessing and realize that it's as a result of this trial that this blessing is coming and thank God for the trial! That's why the Lord said, *"Without a vision my people perish."* Thank God that in His mercy and love He always gives a vision of the victories ahead, the victories coming "as a result of" the trials, and thank God that He also gives His precious promises, which help us to endure and help us to grasp the victories ahead.

I believe that one of the things unusual and great sorrows and trials in a Christian's life brings is a preparation for something great the Lord wants to do in that life or some gift the Lord has to give as a reward, whether it be an earthly reward or a heavenly reward.

We do not gain success if there is nothing to strive against. Therefore we gain success not in spite of the handicaps and trials, but because of them, *as a result of them!* Praise the Lord for His Word! Praise the Lord for His promises!

He Is Worthy

While we sang "Worthy Is the Lamb" one Sunday morning, my spirit soared anew with the realization that "yes, indeed, Jesus is worthy." In thankfulness, my mind began to think of how much He is worthy and indeed how much He is worth *it!* It, being the battles of life when many times discouragement comes to us and we wonder if it is all really worth it!

Indeed, the devil will wage war against us and sometimes it does seem that everything is a battle and that there are endless persecutions. In the heat of battles the enemy may indeed dare to have us wonder sometimes—Is it worth it? But we must remember that the way of the cross leads home. The way of the cross is worth it and it is then that we must remember what Jesus said about counting the cost. In Luke 14, when Jesus speaks to the people in a parable about bearing their cross if they wish to follow Him, He warns that whoever follows Him must first count the cost (Luke 14:27–28).

IS IT WORTH IT—Is it worth it when you're being harassed on the job to stick it out—Yes because of that fat paycheck? Yes because of the bonus? Yes because of the promotion? But more so because your actions are being watched by someone who may turn to Jesus because of your unspoken testimony for Christ before them.

Is it worth it to remain silent when they spit at you and curse you and say all manner of evil things about you? Yes, so that we may know Him and the power of His resurrection—that we may be made conformable to Him through the fellowship of His sufferings (Phil. 3:10) and yes, because of the crown that Jesus will give to us on that blessed day when we come face to face with Him.

Is it worth it when people are telling lies about you and viciously slandering your name—is it worth it to respond in silence when these things are happening in your life? Yes, because God has promised:

Stand still and see the salvation of the Lord (Ex 14:13).
Your God shall fight for you and you shall hold your peace (Ex 14:14).
Be still and know that I am God (Ps. 46:10).
Your enemies shall be found liars unto you (Deut. 33:29).

Is it worth it to give up that piece of pizza or the roast beef or that piece of pie in order to continue on the fast? Yes because of what God will do for me when I complete my covenant with Him! and because He said *"Man shall not live by bread alone but by every word that proceedeth out of the mouth of God"* (Matt. 4:4).

JESUS THINKS I WAS WORTH IT! When Jesus was impaled upon that piece of wood, He thought I was worth it. Jesus stayed upon the cross for me—for my sake, because He thought my salvation was worthy of His sufferings. "He could have called ten thousand angels to destroy the world and set Him free," as the song reminds us. Jesus could have saved Himself at any moment during those excruciatingly painful and terrible hours upon that piece of wood, but He endured it so that we could have eternal life. He allowed His enemies to mock Him and then impale Him upon the plank of wood—He allowed this seeming "failure" situation to occur in His life so that we could win in life—so that we can be winners and reign with Him in life for all eternity—so that we may win! To our Lord, our salvation was worth suffering on the cross.

Paul endured hardships for the elect's sake—Paul thought it was worth it to endure for his brethren's sake (2 Tim 2:10). Many first-century Christians thought it was worth it when they were being led to their deaths to be fed to the lions.

HE IS WORTH IT FOR HE IS WORTHY! When we sing "He is worthy" let us mean it and know what we're saying.

Indeed Jesus is worth suffering for. Jesus is worth going through trials and tribulations for. *". . . great is your reward in heaven . . ."* (Matt. 5:12), (Luke 6:23). Also, as Peter reminds us, a child of God who is suffering ceases from sin, for suffering brings the will of God into our lives. *". . . for he that has suffered in the flesh has ceased from sin"* (1 Pet. 4:1–2).

Jesus is worth going hungry for. *". . . Man shall not live by bread alone but by every word that proceedeth out of the mouth of God"* (Matt. 4:4).

Jesus is worth being cursed for and when the world curses us God blesses us! The words of Ps. 109:28 states: *"Let them curse but bless thou."* When David was being cursed by Shimei in 1 Sam. 16, he said to his servants who wanted to kill Shimei: *". . . Let him alone, and let him curse; for the Lord hath bidden him. It may be that the Lord will look upon mine affliction and that the Lord will requite me good for his cursing this day."* The NIV states: *"It may be that the Lord will see my distress and repay me with good for the cursing I am receiving today."* Christ has redeemed us from the curse of the law anyway and upon the cross Jesus thought we were worth suffering for and indeed I know my Jesus is worthy of all the wrongs the world wants to level at me. He is worthy. Worthy is the lamb that was slain.

I find that when I am being tempted by anger and ill feelings are creeping up on me, it helps me to put back on humility and overcome anger if I can just take this position that Jesus is worthy of all my sufferings, and victory then comes quickly even as I whisper, "Jesus, you're worth it, you're worth going through this for. Lord, I'll do it for you, I'll do it for Heaven's sake; I'll be the way you want me to be for you are more than worth it." If I immediately take this position in my heart, then pride flies away with anger swiftly following and the sweet mantle of humility brings me back to the feet of Jesus.

Yes, Jesus is worth it. He is worthy of all my sufferings; therefore I will rejoice in tribulation, for He is worthy. He is worthy of all the gold of the spirit I can bring to Him. Jesus is worth it for **He is worthy**.

The Trial Has Made Me Good for Something

At Bible study in church tonight we had been taught on the fruit of the spirit—particularly joy. On my way home, with condemnation hitting me hard because of some foolish way I had spoken to someone and the memory of my lack of self-control in the wrath I displayed at work today, I began to feel sorry for myself and feel bad at myself. I forgot temporarily all about confessing, Rom. 8:1–2.

I was caught up in a reverie of years gone by and found myself musing about what I had done and hadn't done for the Lord. In this daydreaming state I became like two people—asking myself questions and answering those questions. I began talking to myself and mused over and over that I really must learn to walk in the spirit more. Then I literally began to beat up on myself by asking, "What things have I done in this world that are good anyway?" "What good have I brought to the world in all my years upon this earth, for instance, who have I brought to Christ?" "If I should be called home to Glory now, what mark would I have left that was good?" In my self-pity I allowed myself to say to myself that I really was good for nothing! [That in itself is a great sin because Jesus living in me has made me something worthwhile. Do I not have His spirit and His glory living in me? Is not the Christ in me the hope of Glory?

69

Is not the King of Glory resident in me? (Dwelling on one's self can make one become morose.)]

In this state, self-pity and condemnation continued. Yes, it's true, I did bring my sister to Christ, but then Dawn would have come to Jesus sooner or later anyway. She was always meant to come to Christ; anyone could tell that. She had never really been the great sinner that I had been before Christ came into my life. So I couldn't boast about bringing Dawn to the Lord. Yes, it's true I did bring others to Christ but they were people I had met momentarily—people I met while travelling, the two men who came to cut my trees when I had the house in Roselle, the man in the car dealership, the woman who gave me a ride to the train station whom I had met at the doctor's office, and a few others, but I never saw them again and so I don't know if that fruit remained. And, of course, I said the prayer of salvation with my children and my grandchildren a few times. Yes, it's true I am a kind and merciful person. I've given away a lot of my monies I've earned to God's work and to God's people and in helping others. Yes, it's true that I've been used in church as a demon chaser, Sunday school nursery worker, typist, etc.

Then I began to think of the fruit of the spirit—what fruit did I have? Yes, I think I have patience, kindness, long-suffering, goodness; and self-pity said, "You would have more love, peace, and joy if it wasn't for this awful trial you've been going through for the last ten years of your life." My big trial! A hint of bitterness is still there. Obviously I have not put it down in the spirit yet! I have not died to it yet! But then if it wasn't for the trial, would I have so much patience, kindness, long-suffering, goodness, etc.? And I must admit the trial has brought to me a certain kind of humility that I didn't have before—I guess that comes with having had to sort of walk with my head emotionally bowed for so long. So this great trial of mine is good for something! And is making my life good for something! And didn't God say to me nine years ago when I asked Him "Why?" that **he was giving me a testimony?** Wasn't His answer to my "Why" that *I am giving you a testi-*

mony"? Didn't He say He was giving me a testimony? Could it be that indeed I have my testimony out of this trial! So I am not such a bad person after all! Yes, it's true that I have written a book glorifying Jesus, and isn't it the trial that has caused me to write this book for the glory of God! *That's good for something!* It's the great trial that's come into my life these past ten years that is making my life good for something after all, and through it all I am getting my gold together for Jesus!

After encouraging myself in this manner, I then began to think that even though the testimony that God is giving me may not be what I thought it would be, indeed, I may never have the type of victory I fantasized about many times ("My thoughts are not your thoughts, my ways are not your ways," saith the Lord), but my victory may be a lot more satisfying—eternally satisfying—for the trial of my faith is more precious than gold and my victory and my testimony will be in the gold of the spirit, which lasts forever.

Zeph. 3:14–20: *Sing, O daughter of Zion; shout, O Israel; be glad and rejoice with all thy heart, O daughter of Jerusalem. The LORD hath taken away thy judgments, He hath cast out thine enemy: the king of Israel, even the LORD, is in the midst of thee: thou shalt not see evil any more. In that day it shall be said to Jerusalem, Fear thou not: and to Zion, Let not thine hands be slack. The LORD thy God in the midst of thee is mighty; he will save, he will rejoice over thee with joy; he will rest in his love, he will joy over thee with singing. I will gather them that are sorrowful for the solemn assembly, who are of thee, to whom the reproach of it was a burden. Behold, at that time I will undo all that afflict thee: and I will save her that halteth, and gather her that was driven out; and I will get them praise and fame in every land where they have been put to shame. At that time will I bring you again, even in the time that I gather you: for I will make you a name and a praise among all people of the earth, when I turn back your captivity before your eyes, saith the LORD.*

71

Rewards from Waiting on the Lord

The end of the Book of Job gives the example of the good end of suffering:

I know that thou cans't do everything and that no thought can be withholden from thee. . . . I have uttered things too wonderful for me which I knew not. . . . I have heard of thee by the hearing of the ear but now mine eye seeth thee. Wherefore I abhor myself and repent in dust and ashes. . . . And the Lord turned the captivity of Job, when he prayed for his friends: also the Lord gave Job twice as much as he had before. . . . So the Lord blessed the latter end of Job more than his beginning.

Paul said, *"These troubles and sufferings of ours are, after all, quite small and won't last very long. Yet this short time of distress will result in God's richest blessing upon us forever and ever"* (2 Cor. 4:17).

The Sermon on the Mount is most comforting to read in times of trials and tribulations. St. Matthew 5:10–12 says:

Blessed are they which are persecuted for righteousness sake for theirs is the kingdom of heaven. Blessed are ye when men shall revile you and persecute you and say all manner of evil against you falsely, for my sake. Rejoice and be exceedingly glad: for great is your reward in heaven: for so persecuted they the prophets which were before you.

In 1 Cor. 9:24, the apostle Paul reminds us that we're rewarded with a prize: *"Know ye not that they which run in a race run all, but one receiveth the prize? So run, that ye may obtain."*

One of the prophecies that the Holy Spirit has given us at church and that I've held onto in the last ten years, goes as follows:

For I order the times and I order the seasons
And I order the days and I order the night
And I order the years
And it is but a small thing for me to order your life
Yield ye unto me, the hand of a great Almighty God
And be ye not discouraged
For I have a time to work in your life
Have faith in me
Do not move to the right nor to the left
For I the Living God will bring it to pass
Saith God

Comforting Words

Here are some precious promises and comforting words that God has given us to hold onto in the race as we run for the gold:

I will never leave you nor forsake you
All things work together for good to those who love the Lord
The joy of the Lord is your strength
Let not your heart be troubled
Nothing shall separate us from the love of God
We are more than conquerors
Greater is He that is in you than he that is in the world
He gives His angels charge over thee
The Lord is the strength of my life
I will go before thee and make the crooked places straight
The eternal God is our refuge and underneath are His everlasting arms
Stand still and see the salvation of your God
Your God shall fight for you and you shall hold your peace
Fear not, O Land, be glad and rejoice for the Lord will do great things
If God be for us, who shall be against us
No weapon formed against thee shall prosper and every tongue that

rises up against thee in judgment thou shall condemn for this is the heritage of the servants of the Lord and their righteousness is of me saith the Lord

When thou passeth through the waters I will be with thee and through the rivers they shall not overflow thee; when thou walkest through the fire thou shall not be burned neither shall the flame kindle upon thee

Being confident of this very thing that He which hath begun a good work in you shall perform it unto the day of Jesus Christ

Be still and know that I am God. I will be exalted amongst the heathen, I will be exalted in the earth; the Lord of hosts is with us, the God of Jacob is our refuge.

In order to live in victory, God's promises must be taken very seriously, for we are indeed more than conquerors and God also says: *"I know the plans I have for you says the Lord. They are plans for good and not evil to give you a future and a hope"* (Jer. 19:11).

Heaven Cheers Us On

In Hebrews 12;1, it is written: *"Wherefore seeing we also are compassed about with so great a cloud of witnesses, let us lay aside every weight, and the sin which doth so easily beset us, and let us run with patience the race that is set before us."*

Even as the Lord commands us to buy for Him gold tried in the fire, I believe that the angels and the spirits of just men made perfect are also cheering us on through our rough waters and thorny pathways as we go for the gold for Jesus and they're saying:

"Jesus is Lord."

"Go on, go on."

"Stay in the running."

"Stay in the race."

"Endure, endure."

"Be a winner."

"Higher, higher."

"Rejoice, rejoice."

"Go for the gold."

"Go for the gold for JESUS."

Hallelujah—Praise the Lord!

I Order The Times

For I order the times and I order the seasons
And I order the days and I order the nights
And I order the years

And it is but a small thing for me to order your life

Yield ye unto me, the hand of a great Almighty God
And be ye not discouraged
For I have a time to work in your life

Have faith in me

Do not move to the right nor to the left

For I the Living God will bring it to pass
saith God

(*Prophecy of the Holy Spirit given at
Deeper Life Christian Fellowship*)

The Prize of the Gold

The prize of the gold is yours
I've already won it for you
I've already gotten you the victory

Just keep on running
Just keep on the right path
Just keep on the right highway

Keep going for the gold

The race is not to the swift
But to he who endures

The prize of the gold is yours

The Dawn of a New Day

Rejoice, Sister
Rejoice, Sister

The mighty hand of the Holy Spirit is upon me

The dawn of a new day will come into your life

And the crying will cease

And the rejoicing will take place

In the name of Jesus

Oh glory, Hallelujah

Praise the Lord!

Prophesied to me by Pastor Sadaphal Sr.
before he went to Glory